DRAW 50

INSECTS

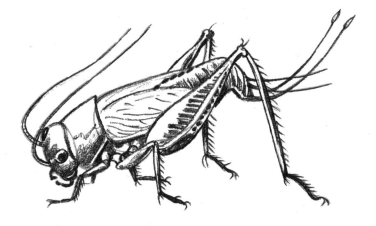

DRAW 50

INSECTS

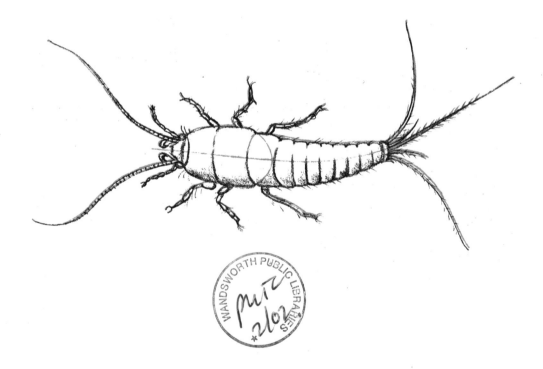

LEE J. AMES with TONY D'ADAMO

KING*f*ISHER

KINGFISHER
Kingfisher Publications Plc
New Penderel House
283–288 High Holborn
London WC1V 7HZ

First published in Great Britain in 1993 under the title
Draw 50 Creepy Crawlies by Kingfisher Publications Plc
Published by arrangement with Doubleday,
a division of Bantam Doubleday Dell Publishing Group, Inc.

10 9 8 7 6 5 4 3 2 1

2TR / 0399 / EDK / HBM(HBM) / 115INST

A CIP CATALOGUE RECORD FOR THIS BOOK IS AVAILABLE FROM THE
BRITISH LIBRARY

ISBN 0 7534 0393 5

Phototypeset by Rowland Phototypesetting Limited,
Bury St Edmunds, Suffolk
Printed in Spain

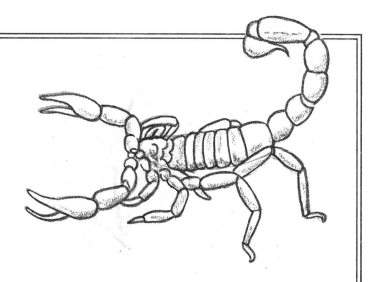

Thanks again, Ray,
for sharing with me your wonderful talent.

L.J.A.

To Lee Ames,
a good friend these many years.

R.B.

TO THE READER

This book will show you a way to draw creepy crawlies. You need not start with the first illustration. Choose whichever you wish. When you have chosen, follow the step-by-step method shown. *Very lightly* and *carefully*, sketch out step number one. However, this step, which is the easiest, should be done most carefully. Step number two is added on top of step number one, also lightly and also very carefully. Step number three is sketched right on top of numbers one and two. Continue in this way to the last step.

It may seem strange to ask you to be extra careful when you are drawing what seem to be the easiest first steps, but this is most important because a careless mistake at the beginning may spoil the whole picture at the end. As you sketch out a step, watch the spaces between the lines, as well as the lines themselves, and see that they are the same. After each step, you may want to lighten your work by pressing it with a plastic, or 'putty' rubber (available at art supply shops).

When you have finished, you may want to redo the final step in India ink with a fine brush or pen—or use a fine pointed felt-tip pen. When the ink is dry, use the plastic rubber to clean off the pencil lines. The rubber will not affect the ink.

Continued over page

Here are some suggestions: In the first few steps, even when all seems quite correct, you might do well to hold your work up to a mirror. Sometimes the mirror shows that you've twisted the drawing off to one side without being aware of it. At first you may find it difficult to draw the egg shapes or circles, or just to make the pencil go where you want it to. Don't be discouraged. The more you practise, the more you will develop control. Use a compass to help you if you wish; professional artists do!

The only equipment you will need will be a medium or soft pencil, paper, the plastic rubber and, if you wish, a compass, pen or brush and India ink–or a felt-tip pen. The first steps in this book are shown darker than necessary so that they can be clearly seen. (Keep your work very light.)

Remember, this book presents only one method of drawing. In a most enjoyable way, it will help you to develop a certain skill and control. But there are many other ways of drawing to which you can apply this skill, and the more of them you try, the more interesting your drawings will be.

Lee J. Ames

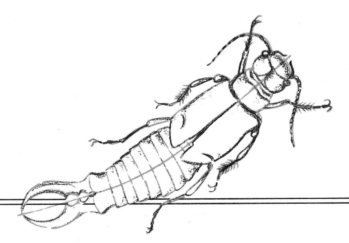

TO THE PARENT OR TEACHER

Drawing, like any other skill, requires practice and discipline. But this does not mean that rewards cannot be found along every step of the way.

While contemporary methods of art instruction rightly emphasize freedom of expression and experimentation, they often lose sight of a very basic, traditional and valuable approach: the 'follow me, step-by-step' way that I learned as a youth.

Just as a beginning musician is given simple, beautiful melodies to play, so too the young artist needs to gain a sense of satisfaction and pride in his or her work as soon as possible. The 'do as I do' steps that I have laid out here provide the opportunity to mimic finished images, images the young artist is eager to draw.

Mimicry is prerequisite for developing creativity. We learn the use of our tools through mimicry, and once we have those tools we are free to express ourselves in whatever fashion we choose. The use of this book will help lay a solid foundation for a child, one that can be continued with other books in the *Draw 50* series, or even used to complement different approaches to drawing.

Above all, the joy of making a credible, attractive image will encourage the child to continue and grow as an artist, giving him even more of a sense of pride and accomplishment when his friends say, 'Peter can draw a butterfly better than anyone else!'

Lee J. Ames

Have fun with
your drawings . . .

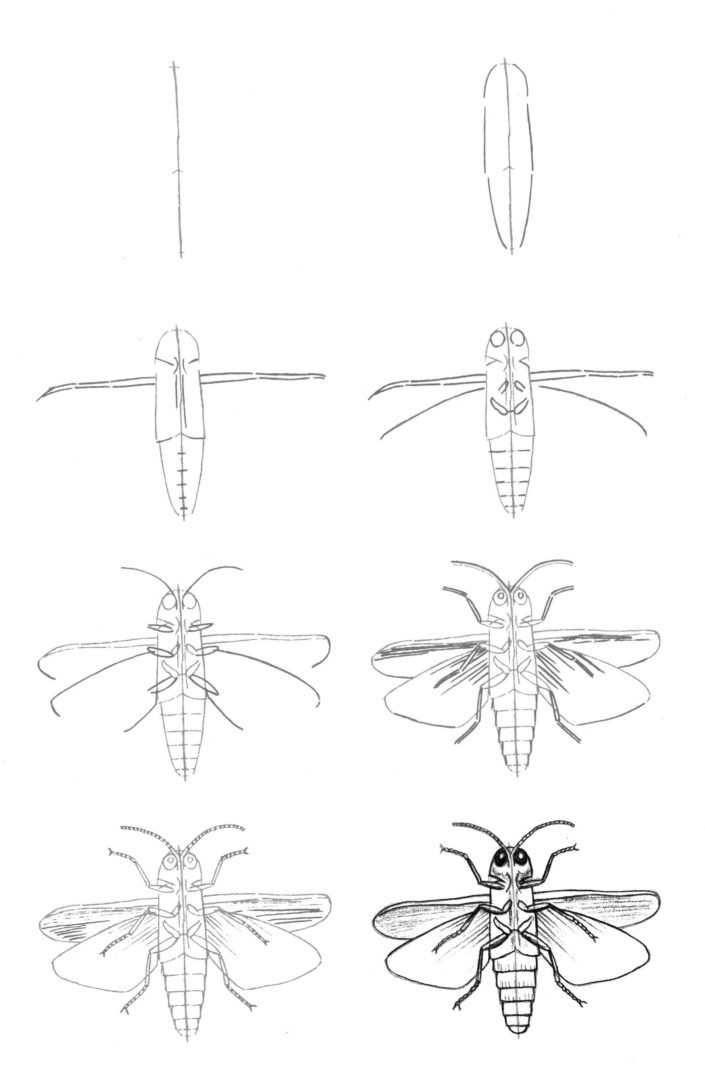

Firefly

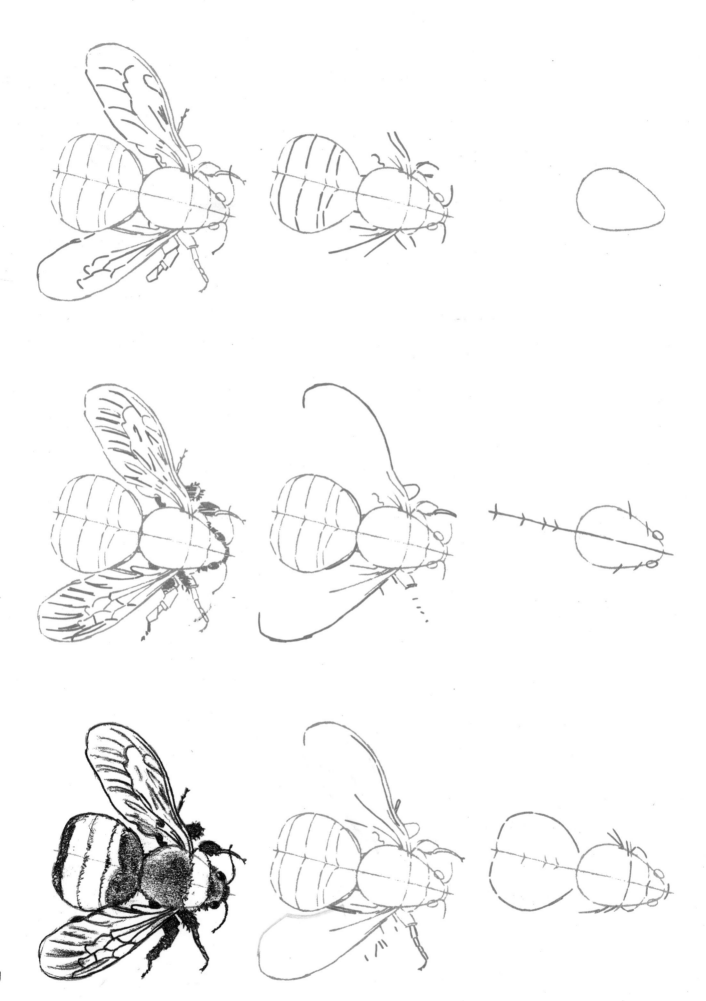

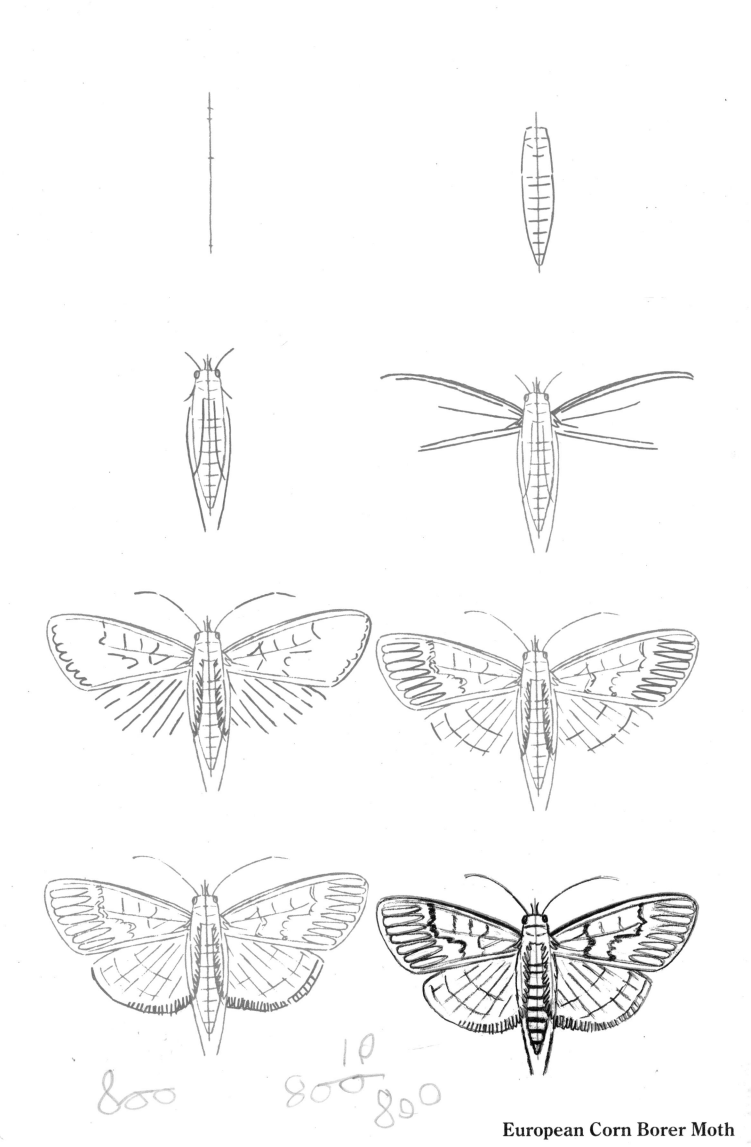

European Corn Borer Moth

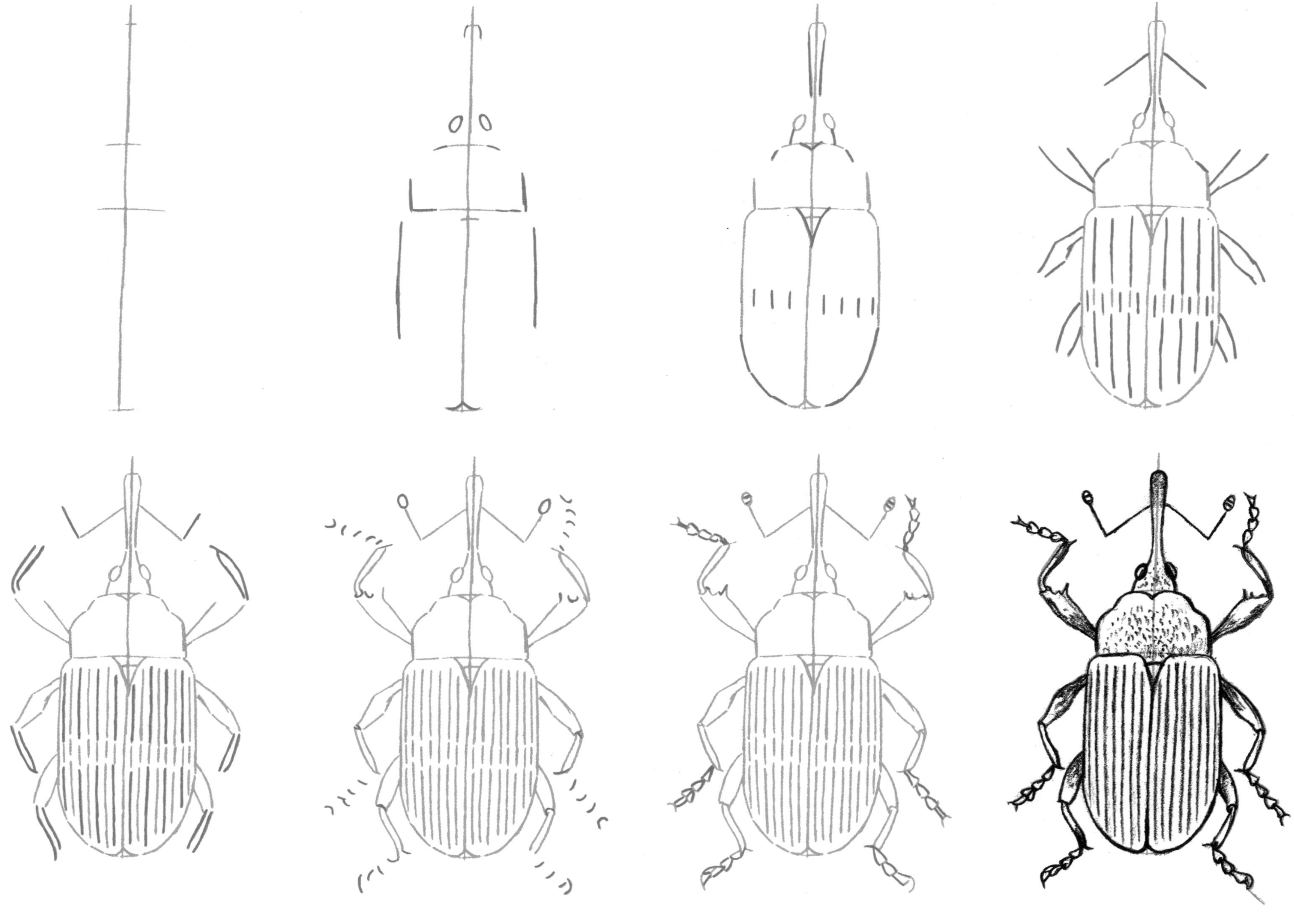

Boll Weevil

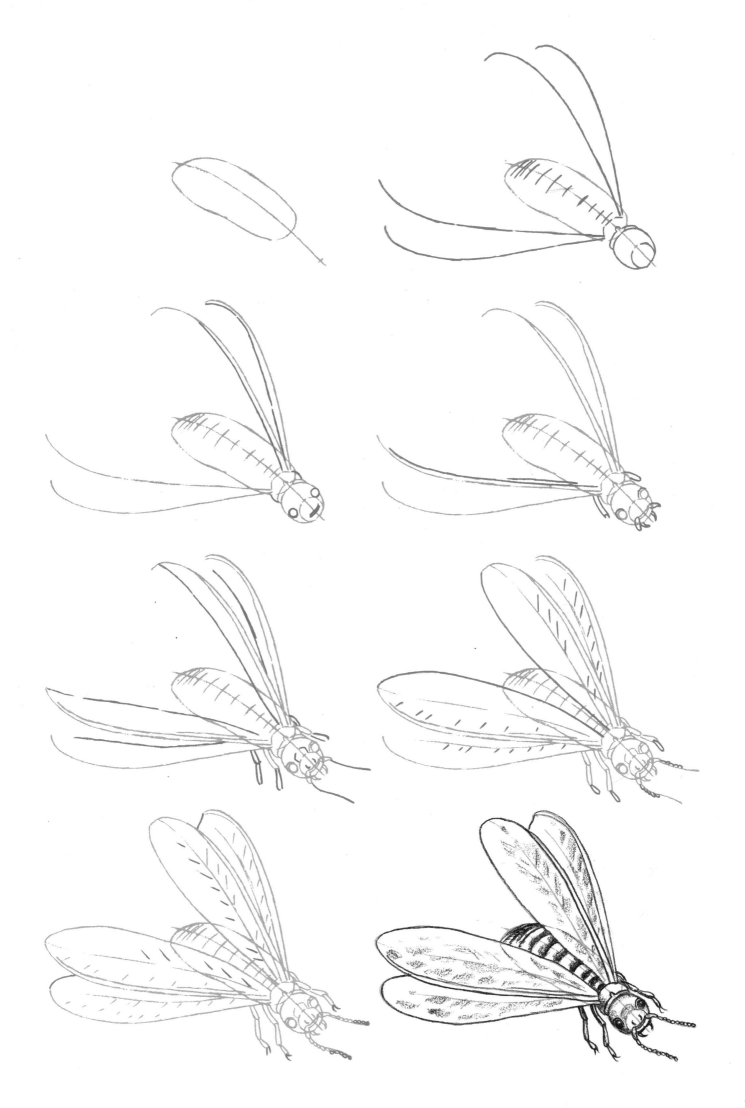

Winged Termite

Japanese Beetle

Anopheles Mosquito

Gypsy Moth Larva

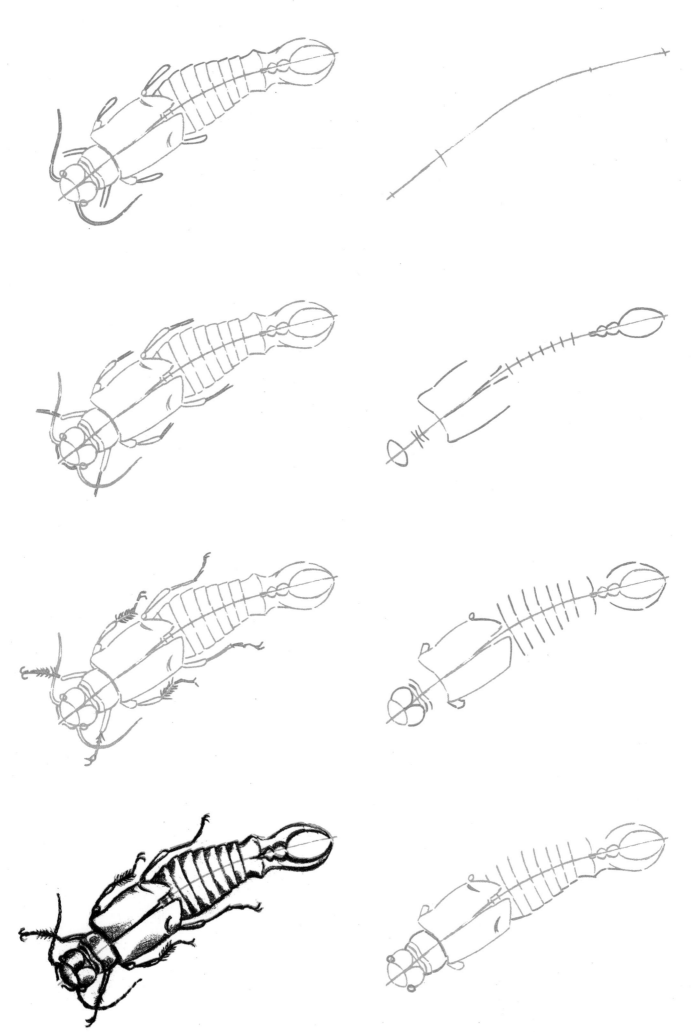

Unicorn Beetle

Assassin Bug

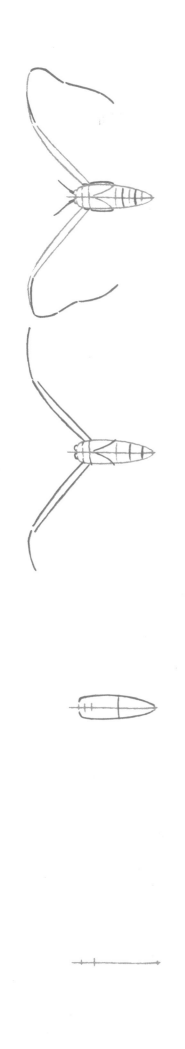
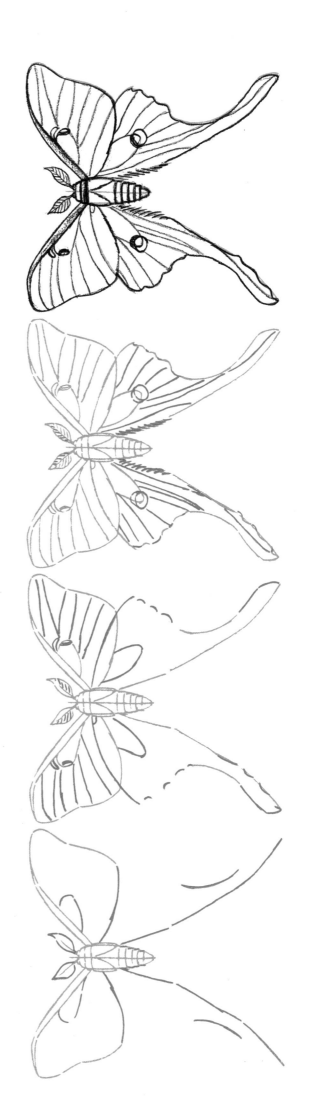

Luna Moth

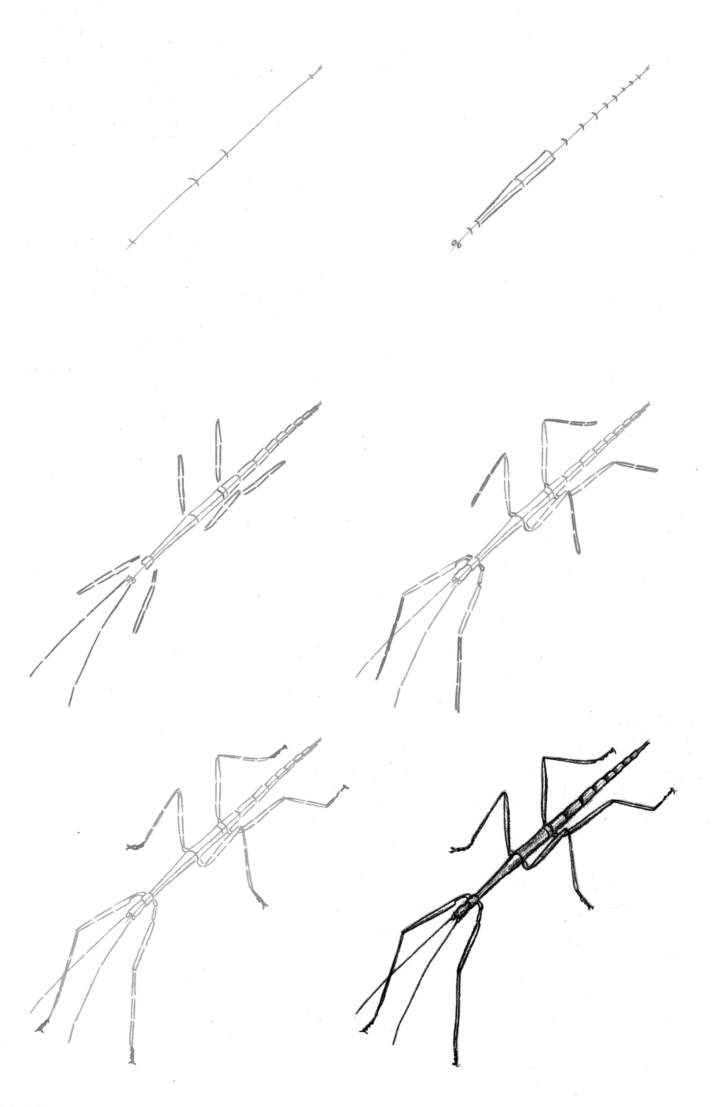

Stick Insect

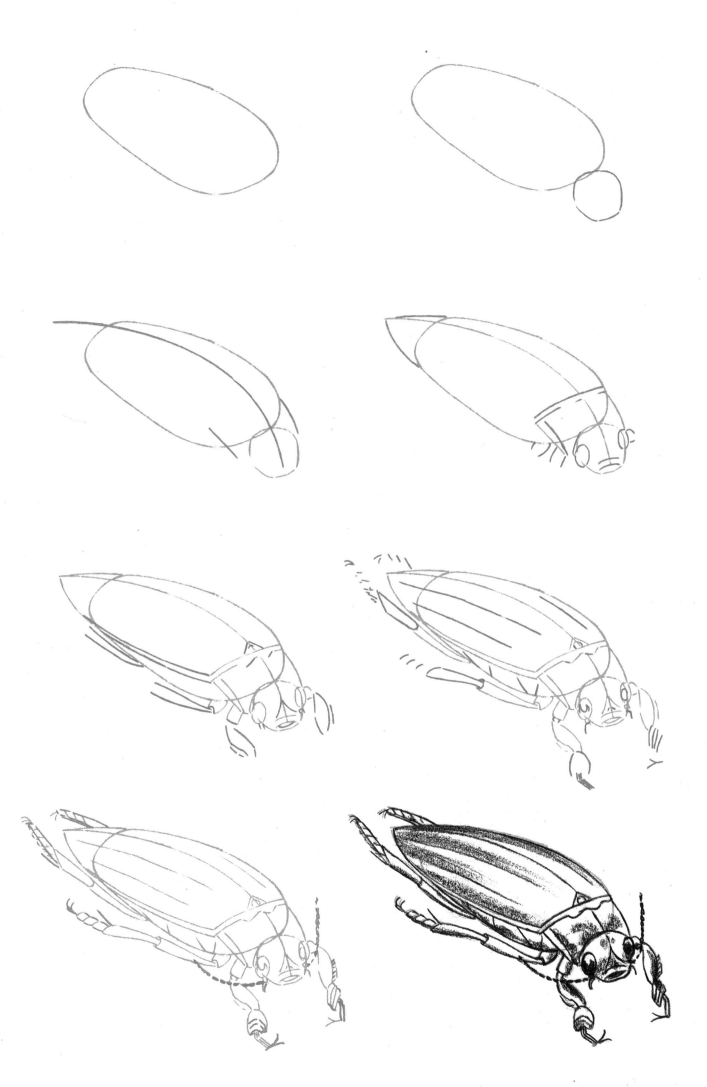

Diving Beetle

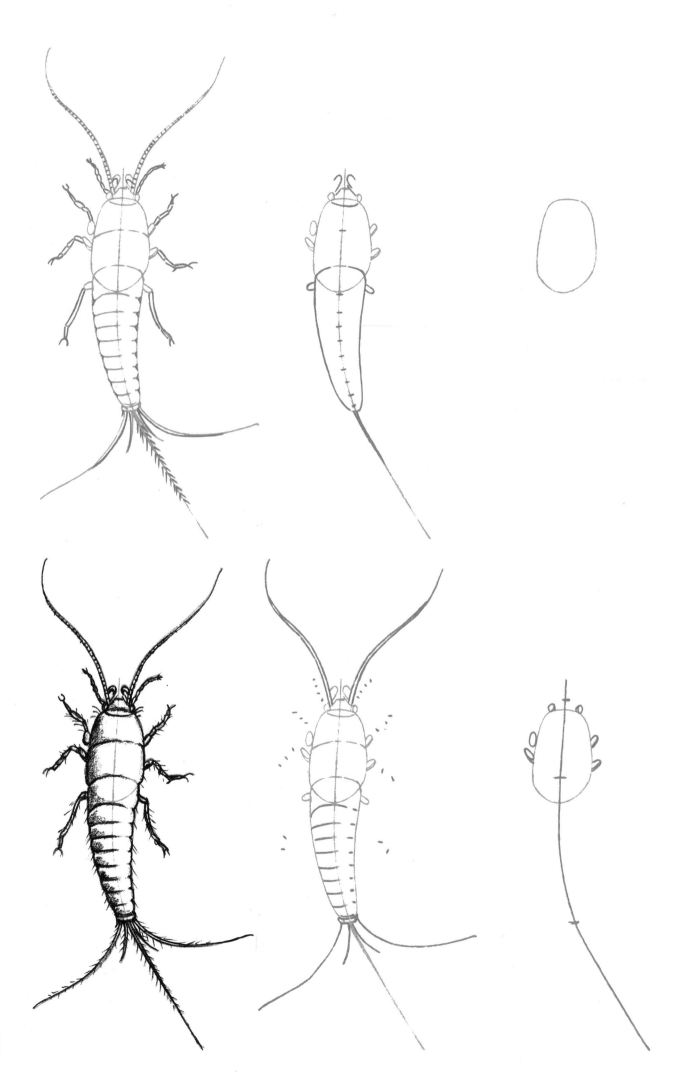

Silverfish

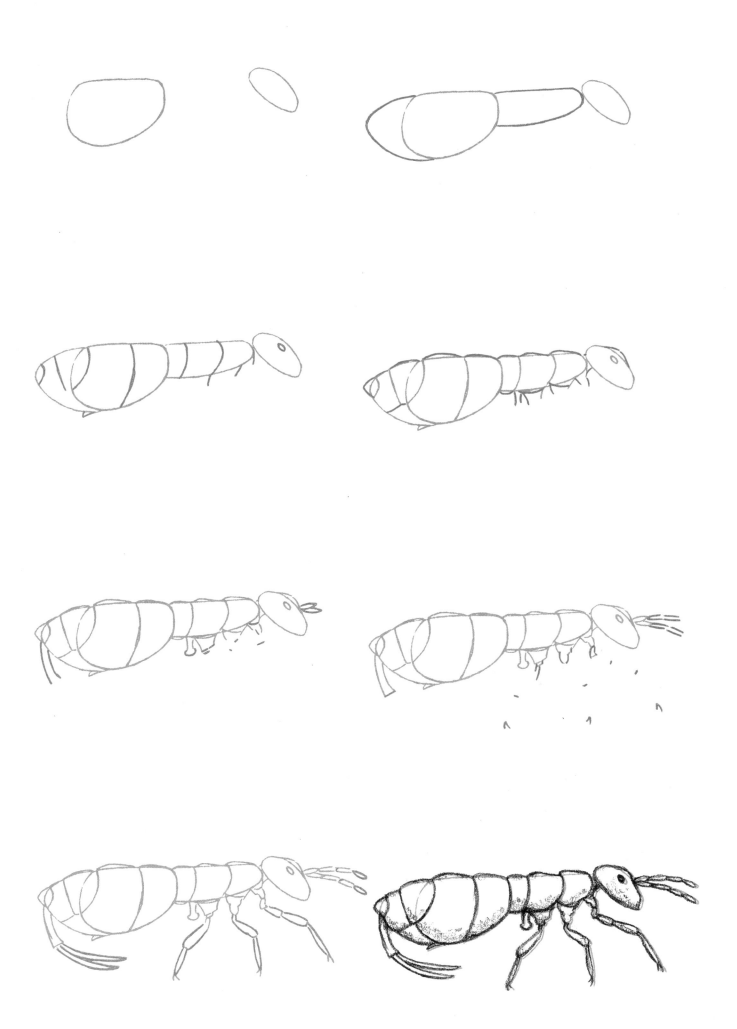

Springtail

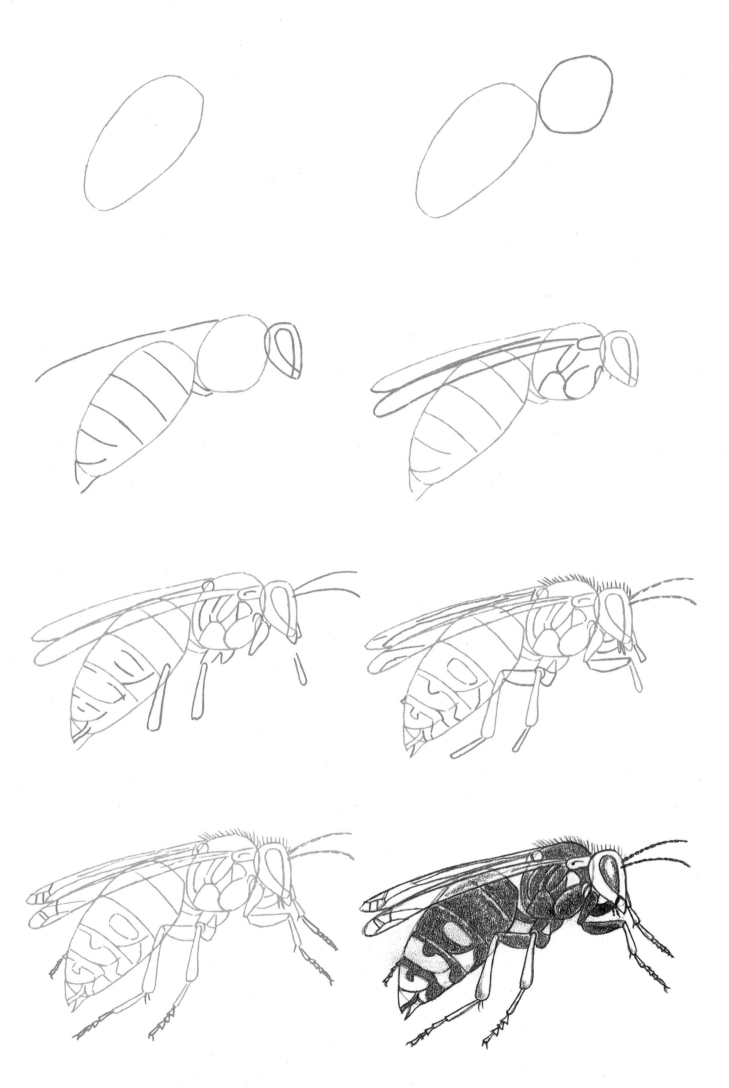

Bald-Faced Hornet

Grasshopper

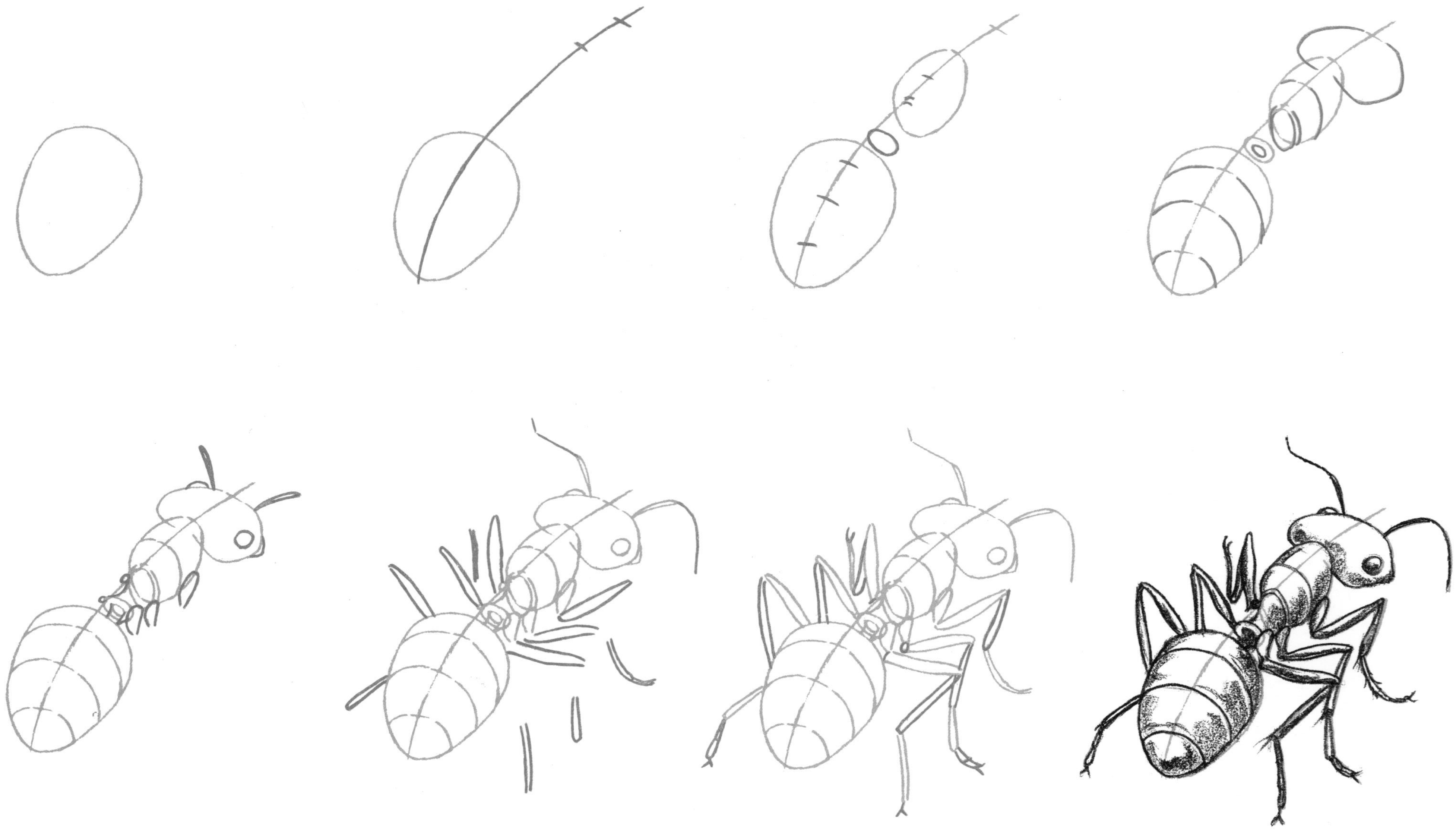

Carpenter Ant

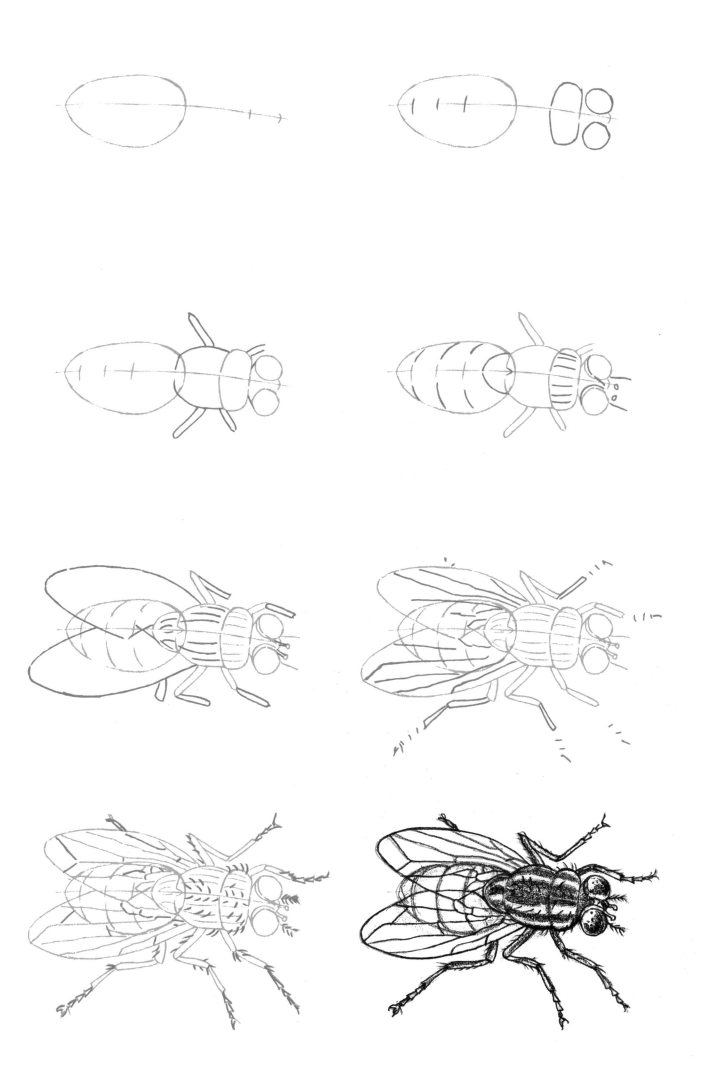

Housefly

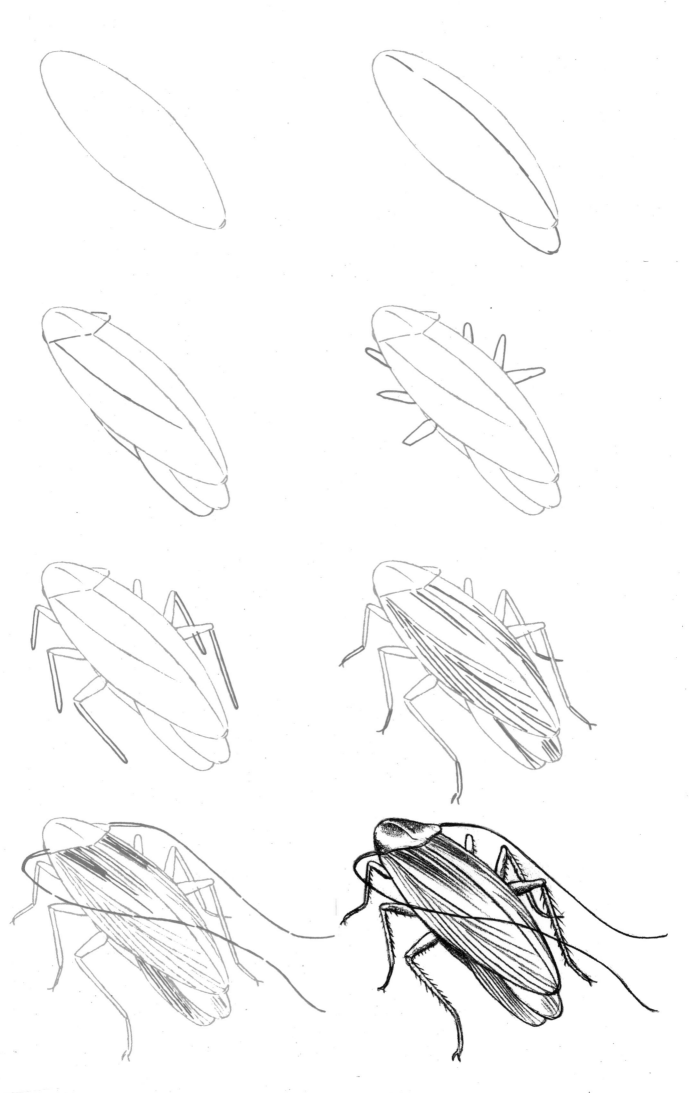

American Cockroach

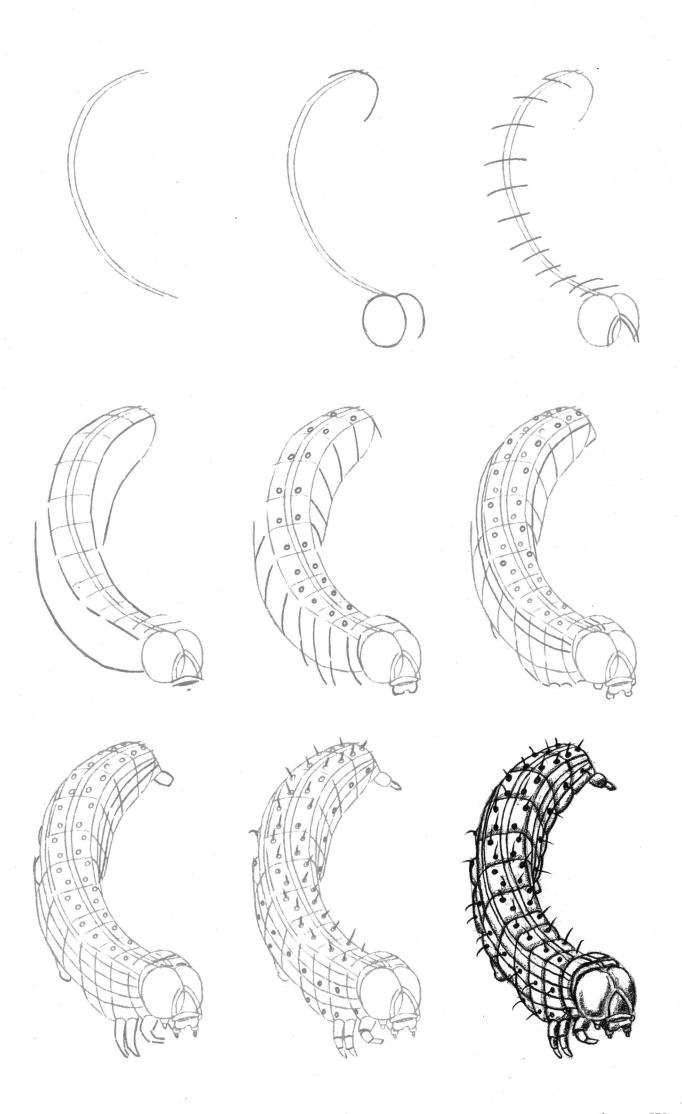

Army Worm

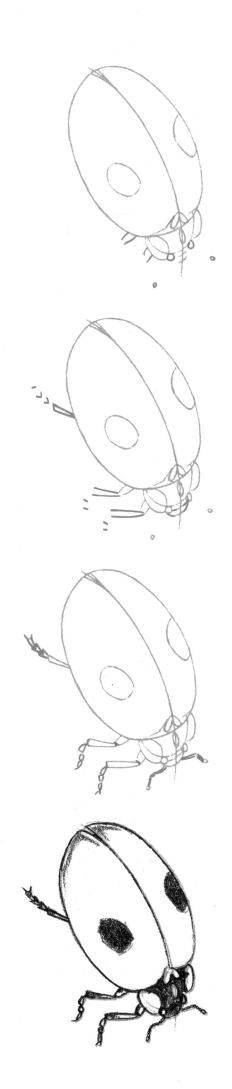
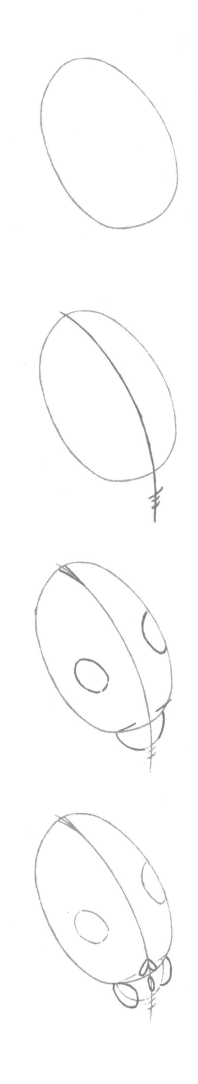

Ladybird

Dragonfly

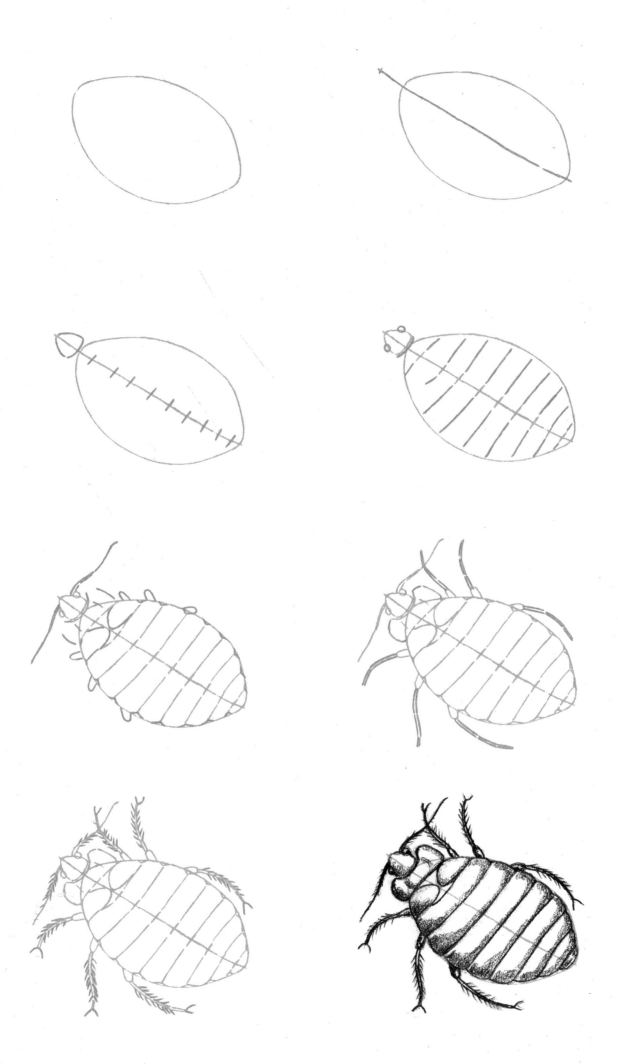

Bedbug

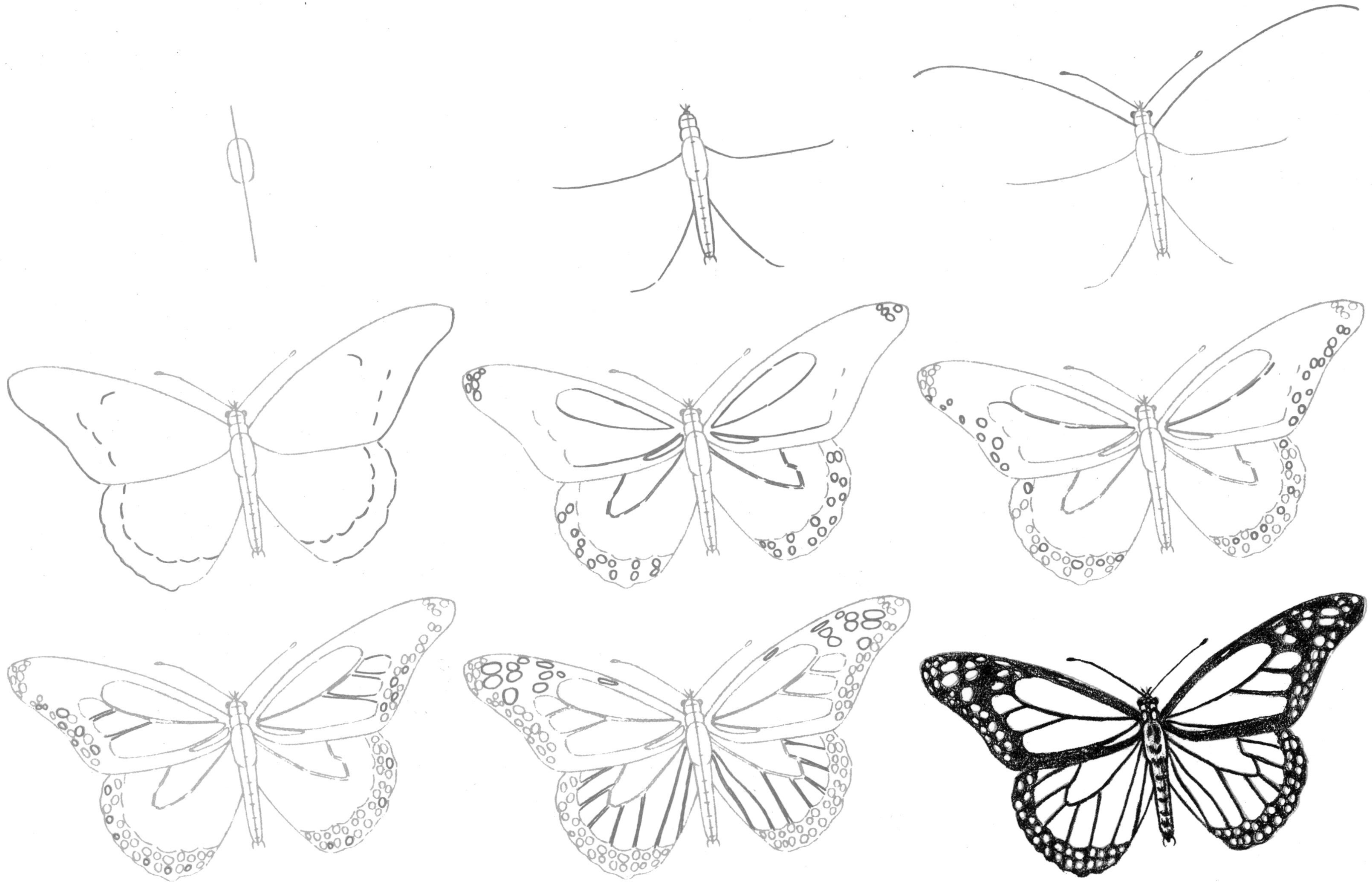

Butterfly

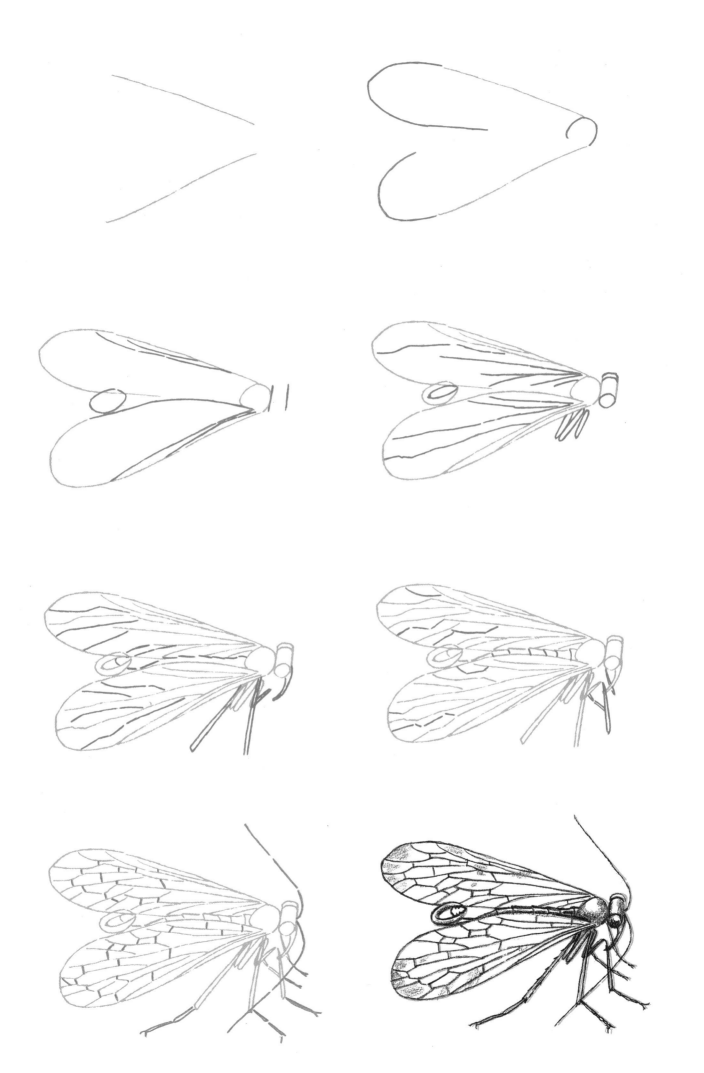

Scorpion Fly

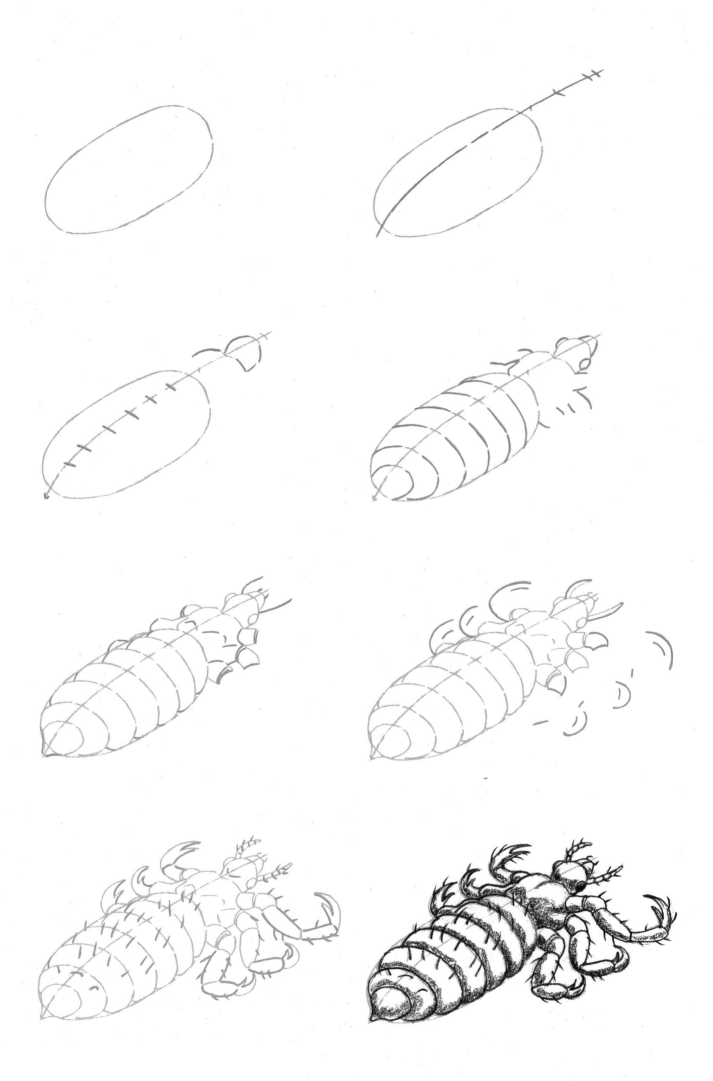

Head Louse

Horntail

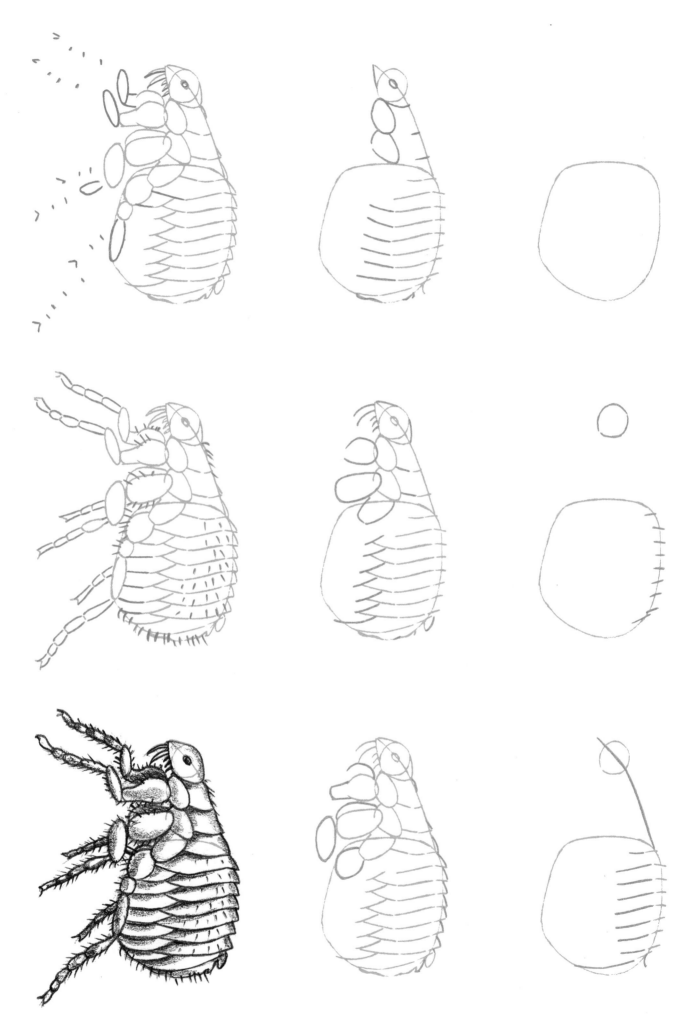

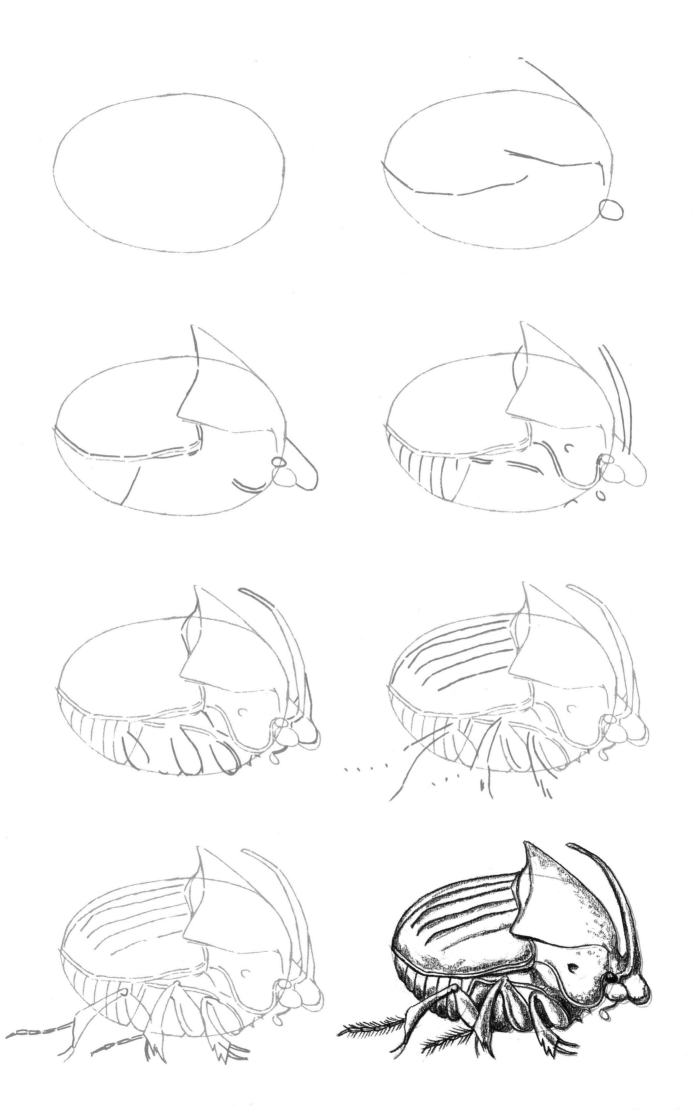

Dung Beetle

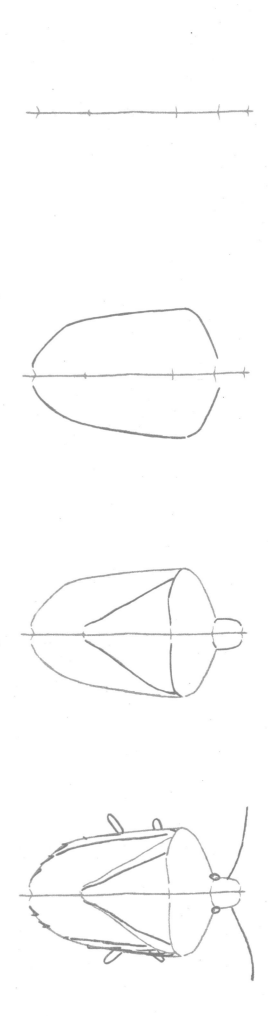

Shieldbug

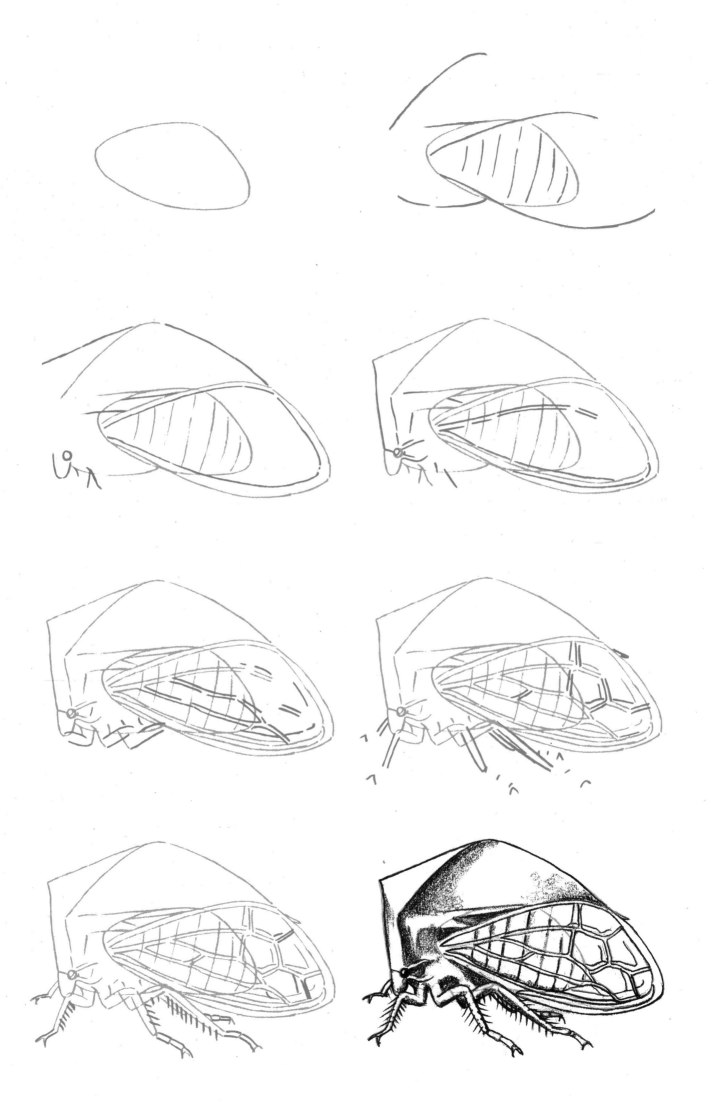

Buffalo Treehopper

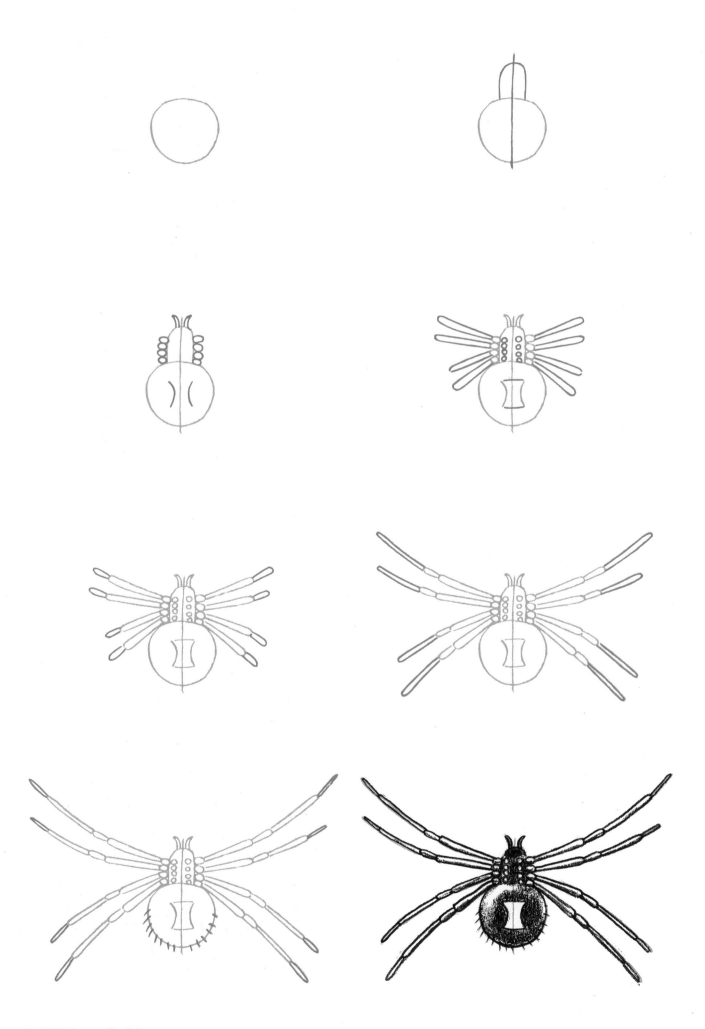

Black Widow Spider

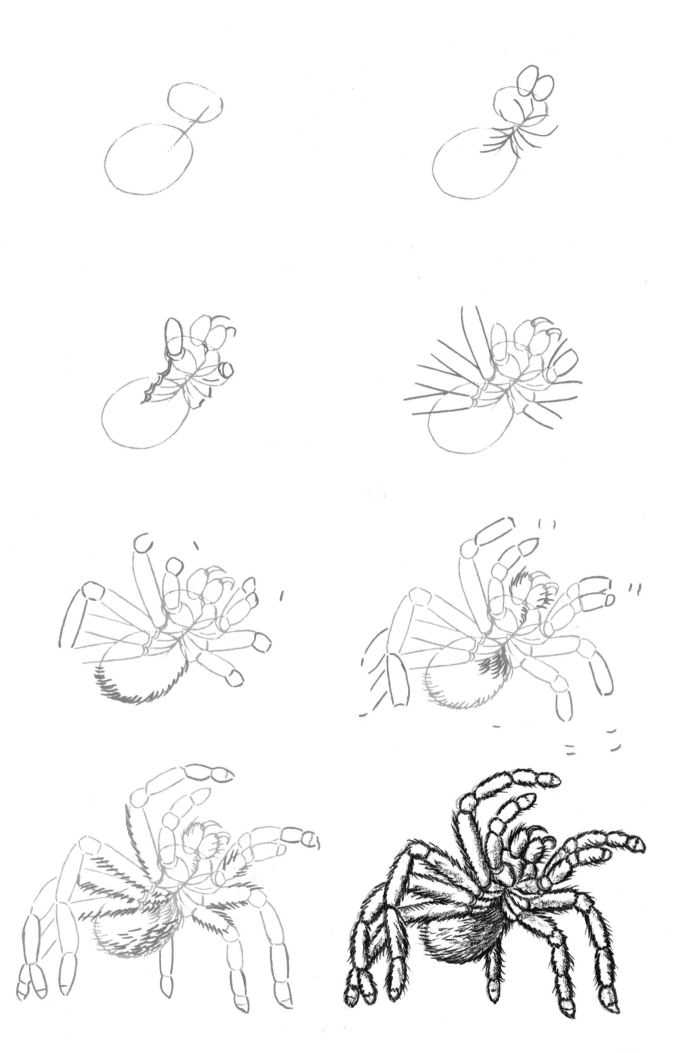

Tarantula

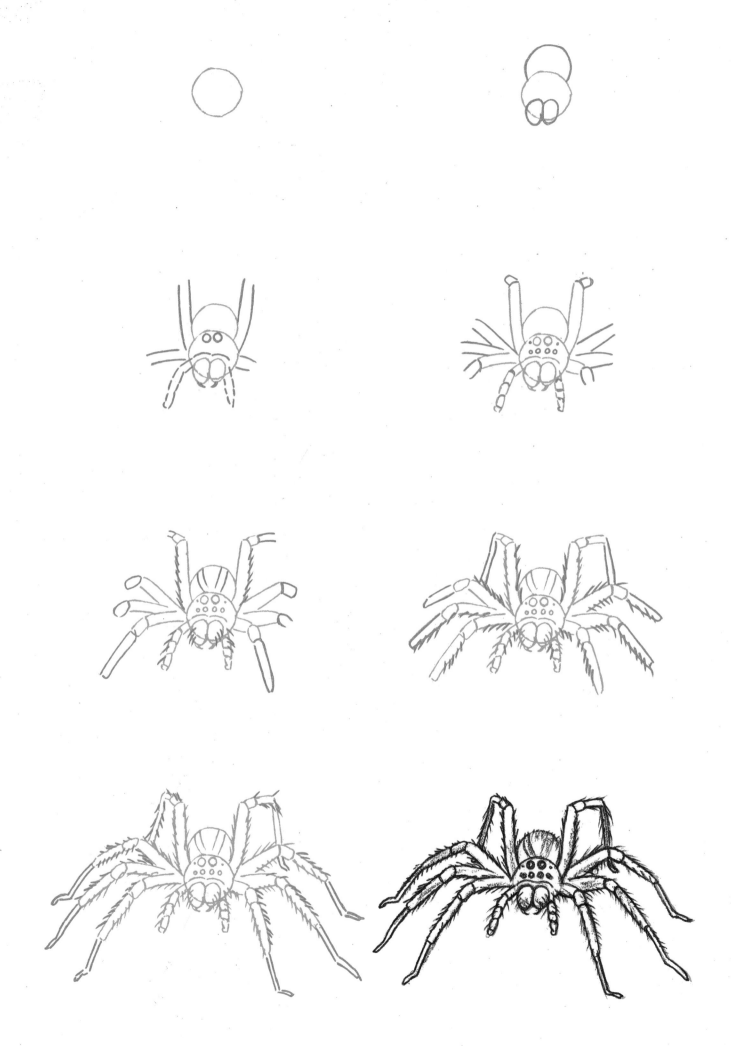

Wolf Spider

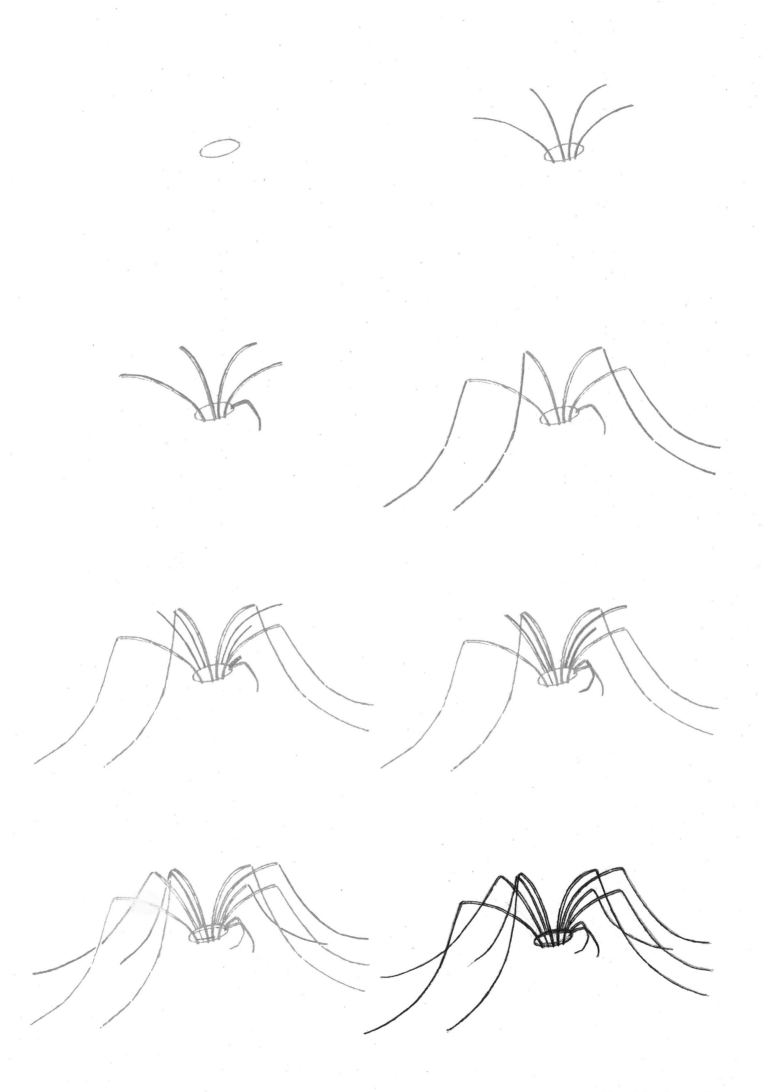

Daddy-long-legs

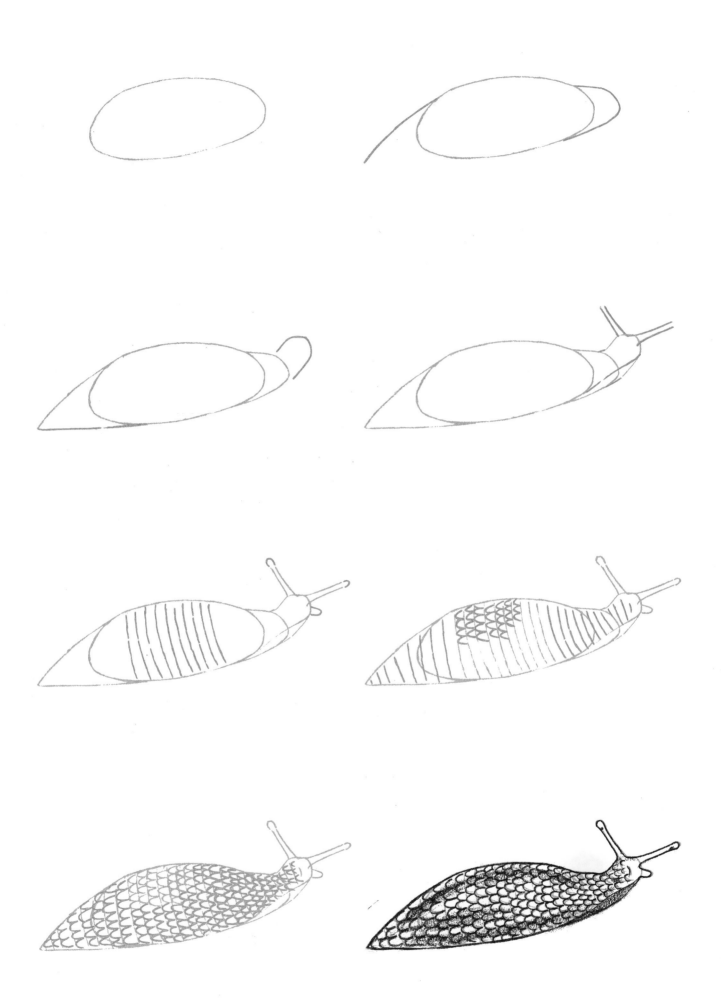

Slug

Snail

Scorpion

Millipede

Centipede

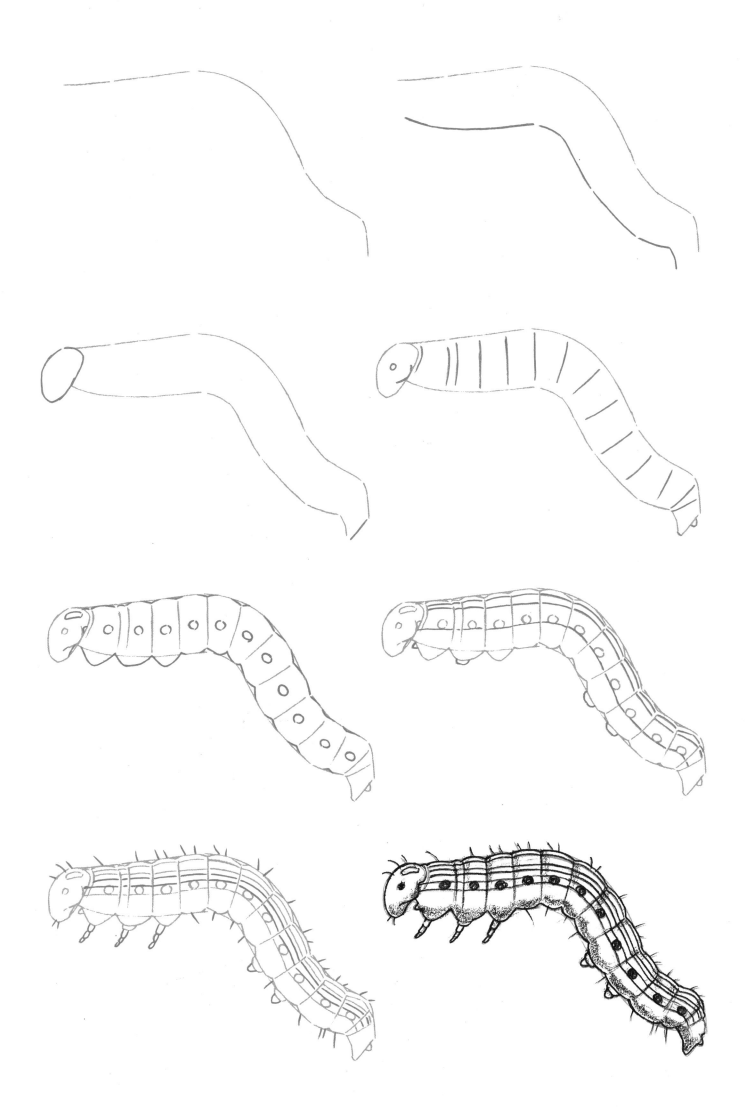

Caterpillar

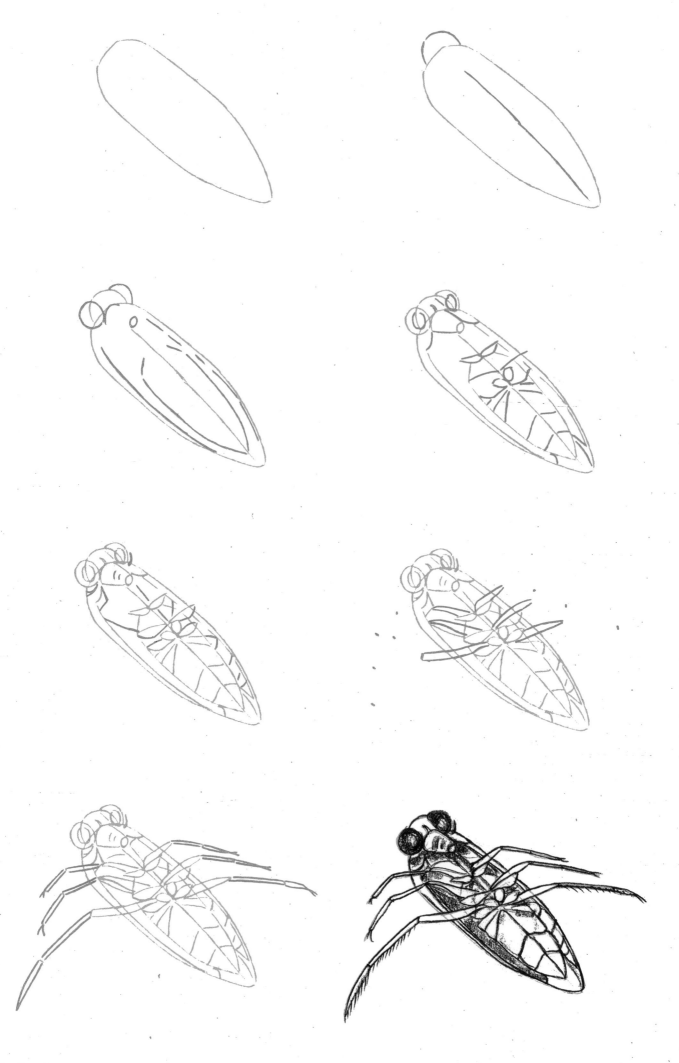

Back Swimmer

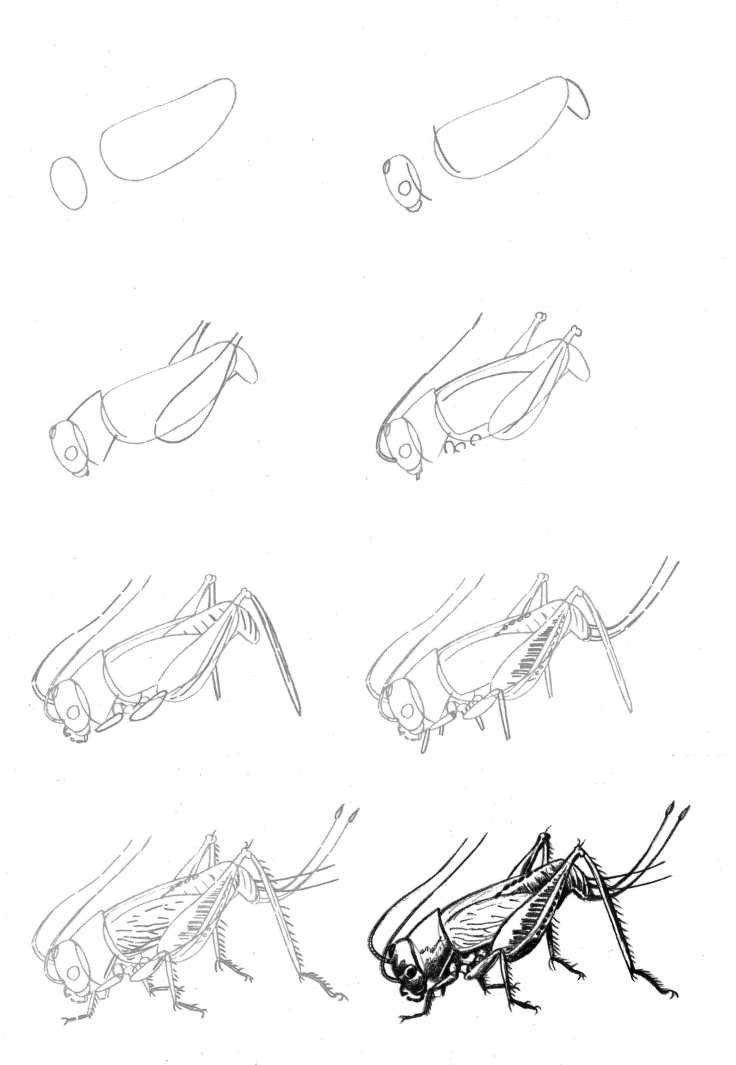

Field Cricket

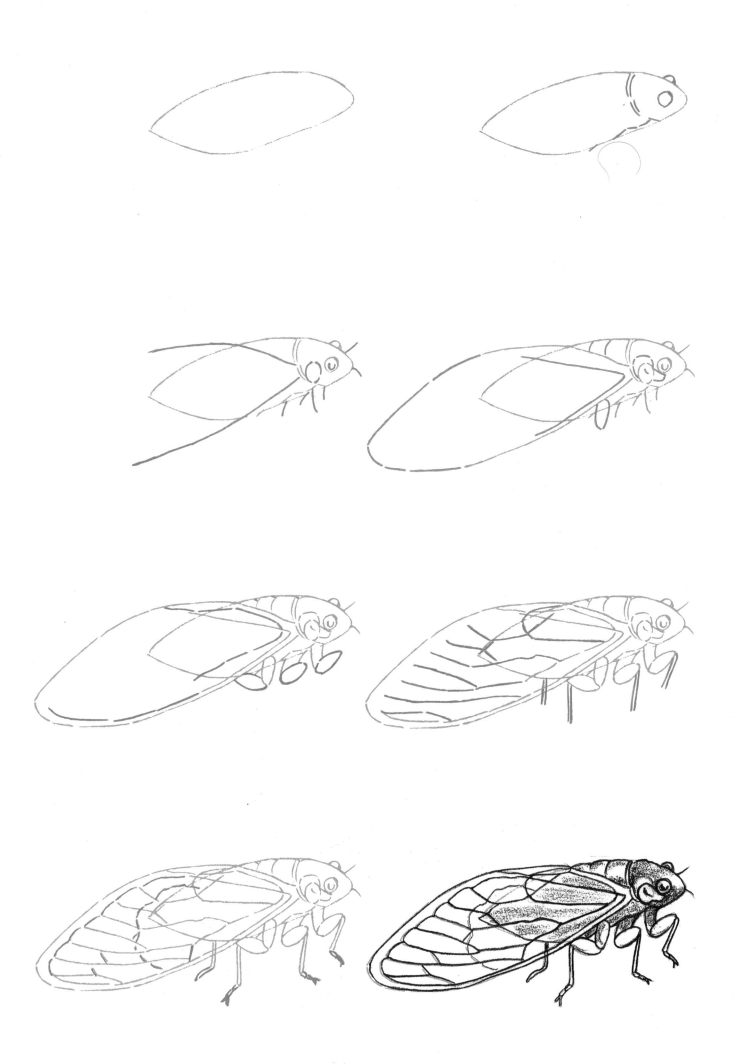

Cicada

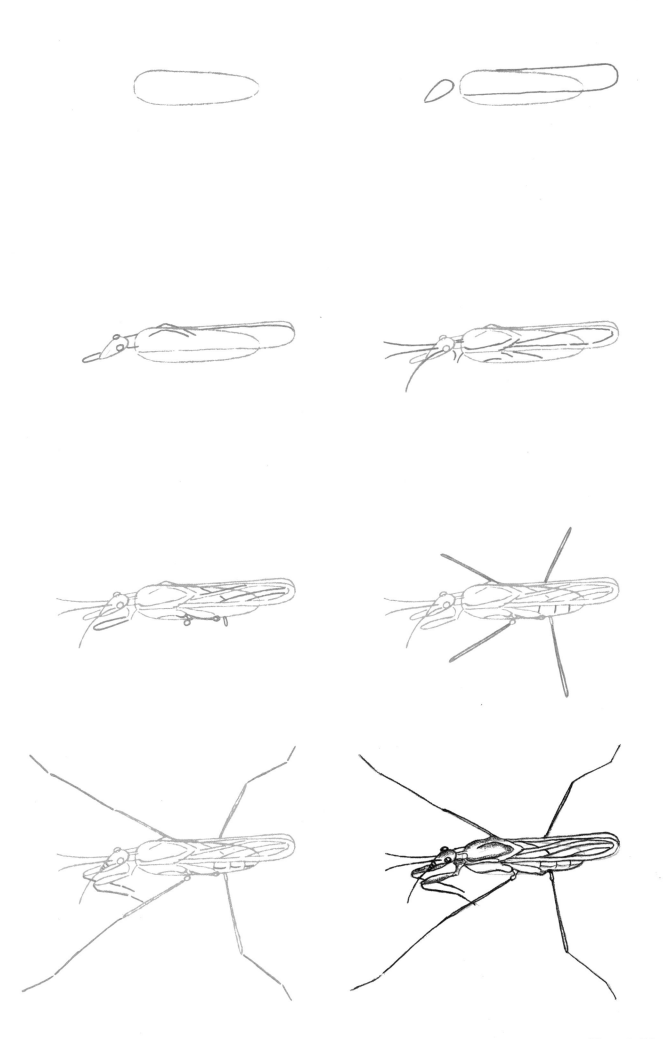

Pond Skater

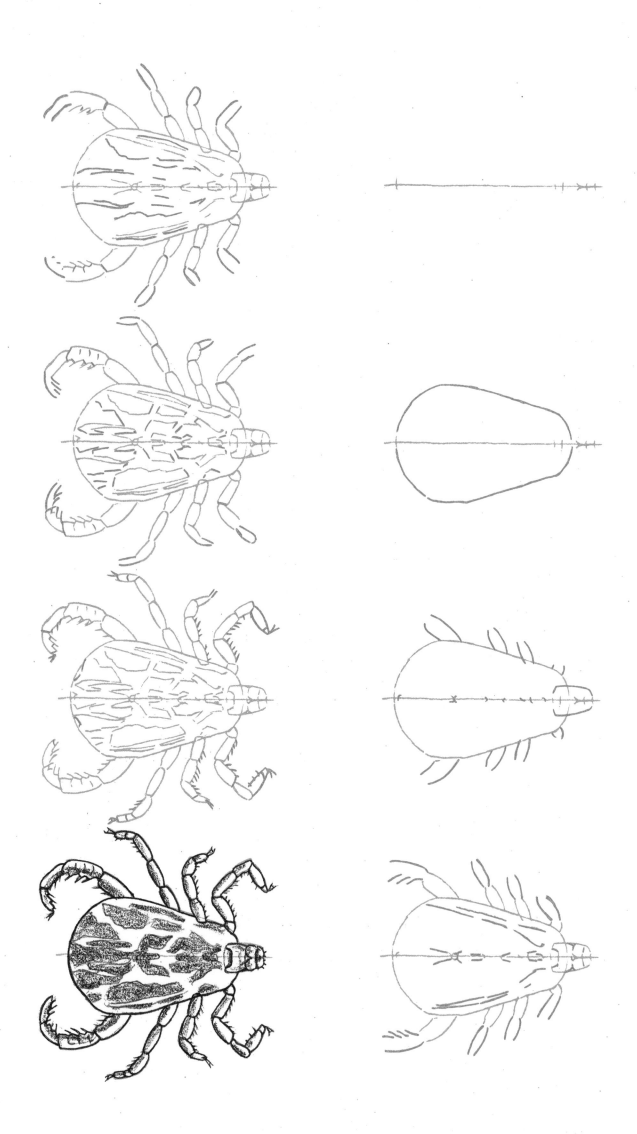

ABOUT THE AUTHOR

Lee J. Ames has been earning his living as an artist for almost forty years. He began his career working on Walt Disney's *Fantasia* and *Pinocchio*. He has taught at the School of Visual Arts in New York City and, more recently, at Dowling College on Long Island, New York State. He was, for a time, director of his own advertising agency and illustrator for several magazines. Mr Ames has illustrated over one hundred books, from preschool picture books to postgraduate texts. When not working, he battles on the tennis court. A native New Yorker, Lee J. Ames lives in Dix Hills, Long Island, with his wife, Jocelyn, their three dogs, and a calico cat.

Ray Burns has worked as a freelance illustrator since 1966. During that time he has illustrated nearly seventy children's books and has worked as a cartoonist. An ex-naval officer, Ray currently lives in Wilton, Connecticut, with his wife and their three children.